Which word Shall I Use?

Marisa Dunn

Acknowledgements

I dedicate and give thanks first to God, our Father in Heaven, for the knowledge and gift to finally produce this book to be a blessing to others. I thank my daughter, Petrice, who is my loyal supporter, always believes in me, and is a fountain of inspiration, support and encouragement, and to Timothy Hudnell, thank you for your sense of humour and wisdom to just let me write.

For Aniyah and Aliyah, who besides their mummy, are two of the most precious and special little ladies in my life and a constant source of energy, hilarity, surprise and wonder. Let us all see life through the eyes of a child.

Introduction

This book, written for the UK market, is a reference book intended to be a source of knowledge and help for those that may not know or understand the difference between words that sound the same but either have a different spelling and meaning or are spelled the same but have different meanings. The book is in alphabetical order making it easy access to find a particular word being searched for and in most cases there are clear explanations and examples in how to use these words. Towards the end of the book are some examples on homonyms.

This is by no means an exhaustive book on homophones or homonyms and there will be some I have missed which are not in this book; nor is this book a piece of literary genius for those that are pedantic. It is simply intended to be used by anyone, whether a student in education, a reader or someone wanting to gain understanding, it's even a useful reference tool for crossword lovers. I hope you will enjoy it and find it very helpful.

ISBN 978 1 326 61724 0

Contents

A
Add-Ad
Ad is short for advertisement and advertising.
Add is to count, to combine, to total an amount up.
Add is to join, insert, improve, complement or increase the amount, size or quantity of something.

Aide-Aid (See Assistance)
Aide is a person who is an assistant, a helper, or supporter; such as, a teacher's assistant, a health care assistant, an assistant manager, or a personal assistant. The word comes from the term *Aide-de-camp*, a person who acts as an assistant.
Aid means to help; to give assistance; to support; to lend a hand; to give food, clothing and shelter to those in need. To give charitable **aid**.

Air-Heir
Air is the atmosphere surrounding us that we breathe, mainly oxygen.
Heir is a relative or a person entitled to inherit goods or money that a deceased person has left to them.

Aisle-Isle-I'll
Aisle is the gangway or walkway between a row of seats in a church. The bride looked lovely as she walked up the **aisle**.
Isle means Island. An island is land that is surrounded by water. Britain is an island, the British **Isle's**.
I'll is a contraction; it is a shorter way of saying, 'I will.'

Ail-Ale
Ail is to be ill or unwell.
Ale is another name for beer. My granddad enjoys his pint of **ale**.

All-Awl
All means the whole amount of everything or everyone.
Awl is a tool used by shoemakers to pierce holes in leather.

Alms-Arms
Alms are given as charity such as shelter, money, clothes, or food for the poor or needy. It was a term used more in the 1800s or earlier where beggars would shout out '**alms** for the poor.'
Arms are the upper limbs on the human body to which the hands are attached.

Allowed-Aloud
Allowed is to grant, permit or to let. 'Yes you are **allowed** to have a day off.'
Aloud is when you are talking loudly not in a quiet voice or a whisper, 'She read the poem out **aloud**.'

Allude-Elude

Allude means to hint at something.

Elude means to avoid, evade, escape from, or dodge; it also refers to puzzle, confuse, and baffle.

Alter-Altar

Alter is to change something, to become different or to vary it. 'I have to **alter** the dress I bought to fit me better.'

Altar is found in churches; it is the holy table used in religious services. After becoming engaged, they were married at the **altar**.

Ante-Anti

Ante in poker is an amount of money put forward by the players before the deal.

Ante is a prefix which goes in front of a word and means, before, prior to.

Antenatal is before the birth and relates to pregnancy.

Anti means against or opposed to something.

Area-Aria

Area refers to a geographical region, surface, size, and place. It is an expanse or measure of a surface; the desert is a vast **area** of sand: 'the **area** right here in my garden is where I am going to plant vegetables.'

Aria is the name for a solo in an opera.

Arc-Ark

Arc is a curve, as in the curve of an arch or circle.

Ark is the boat that Noah built and lived in with his family and animals while it rained for 40 days and 40 nights.

Ascent-Assent

Ascent is to rise, to move upwards, to climb upwards.

Assent is to be in agreement, to agree something to be true, to give consent or permission, to show approval.

Assistance-Assistants (See Aide)

Assistance is to aid, assist, support, contribute, or to give charitably to those in need of help.

Assistants are people who help and assist, particularly in employment where there are shop **assistants**, health care **assistants**, **assistant** managers, or personal **assistants**.

Attendance-Attendants

Attendance is to be physically present, to turn up, to be in **attendance.**

Attendants are helpers, people who may accompany a person or assist or guide by providing a service, such as a porter, waitress, helper, warden.

Ate-Eight
Ate is to have eaten food; 'I **ate** earlier.'
Eight is the number that comes after seven and before nine. 'Seven, **Eigh**t, Nine.'

Aural-Oral
Aural is to do with the ears.
Oral pertains to the mouth. **Oral** is to speak.

Auricle-Oracle (See Oracle)
Auricle is the outer part of the ear.
Oracle is the word of God, the most Holy place in the temple, an answer to something asked.
To consult the **oracle**.

Auger-Augur
Auger is a drill for boring holes.
Augur was a person who predicted the future in the days of the Romans. The **augur** would tell of future events by watching the flight of birds.

Aye-Eye-I (See Eye and I)
Aye is a dialect for yes.
Aye Aye captain is a response given to an order to be carried out in Naval language.
Eye is an organ of sight.
Eye is the hole in a needle that the cotton is thread through.
I refers to oneself, 'me myself and **I**.'

B
Bale-Bail
Bale is a large bundle of straw; a **bale** of hay.
Bale is to jump out of an aeroplane by parachute.
Bale is to remove water leaking into a boat.
Bail is money that is sometimes set for a person to return to court or for the release of a prisoner.

Bald-Bawled (See Bawl)
Bald is to have very little or no hair.
Bawled is to have cried, sobbed, wailed loudly; 'the baby **bawled** his eyes out.'

Ball-Bawl (See Bawled)
Ball is a round object used in sports or games such as football or tennis.
Ball is a social dance or gathering. 'I am attending the **ball** tonight in my beautiful **ball** gown.'
Bawl is to cry, to sob, to wail loudly.

Band-Banned

Band is a flexible narrow strip of rubber or elastic that holds things together; an elastic **band**; a rubber **band**; a hair **band**.

Band is a group of musicians who play music together.

Band is a group of people uniting for the same purpose; **band** of thieves.

Banned is to disallow, prohibit, stop, forbid. 'He is **banned** from playing football.'

Bare-Bear

Bare means naked, to be unclothed, exposed and without cover.

Bear is an animal such as Polar **bears**, Brown **bears**, and Panda **bears**. A child's toy is a teddy **bear**.

Bear is to carry mentally or physically; to endure or to show good results, to **bear** fruit; to **bear** in mind; to **bear** witness to something; to **bear** suffering.

Bard-Barred

Bard is a poet, a lyricist. One who composes and recites lyrics.

Barred means to prevent entry or exit, to forbid, to refuse. 'The streets are **barred** off we cannot enter them: he was refused entry because he was **barred**.'

Barren-Baron

Barren means unable to produce offspring, to be infertile, unfruitful, sterile, unproductive.

Barren land is land which is unfruitful, sterile, uncultivated; a desolate waste.

Baron is the title of nobility; a nobleman.

Base-Bass

Base is the bottom part on which something stands or rests upon. It is the foundation, the lowest part or position, the supporting structure.

Base is an underpinning fundamental principle; 'I **base** my opinion on what I have experienced: I **base** his innocence on the alibi he gave.'

Base is the starting point, the main part, ingredient or element, 'my body lotion has an oil **base**.'

Base is a military camp, such as an army **base**, a naval **base** or an air force **base**.

Bass is a deep, low tone in music or a deep singing voice.

Bask-Basque

Bask is to lie in a warm pleasant environment; to sunbathe; to **bask** in the sun.

Basque is a piece of women's clothing. It is a tight fitting bodice or lingerie.

Basque is a region in Spain.

Beat-Beet

Beat is to physically hit or to strike out.

Beat is the rhythm in music. The rhythm of a drum is called a drum **beat**.

Beat is used in competitive terms to defeat. I want to **beat** my opponent in the race.

Beat means to overcome something; 'I am determined to **beat** my fear of heights.'

Beet is a vegetable; sugar is produced from sugar **beet**.

Beach-Beech
Beach is the seashore, which is sandy and sometimes covered in pebbles.
Beech is a tree. A lot of furniture is made from **beech** wood which is light in colour.

Be-Bee
Be is to exist or to occur; it is used to form certain tenses of verbs; to let it **be**; to **be** there.
Bee is an insect that produces honey; the honey **bee**.

Bean-Been
Bean is a vegetable such as a broad **bean**, or a kidney **bean**.
Been is past of be; 'I have already **been** there.'

Beer-Bier (See ale)
Beer is an alcoholic drink such as ale and lager.
Bier is a stand or framework on which coffins are placed.

Berry-Bury
Berry is a small pulpy fruit, such as a, straw**berry**, Rasp**berry**, or a Goose**berry**.
Bury means to cover, conceal, dispose of; to place in the ground and cover with earth; inter into the ground.

Bell-Belle
Bell is a cup shaped instrument that makes a musical note when struck, such as church **bells**.
Bell also refers to a door**bell**, when pressed it produces a loud sound or musical notes to let the person know someone is at their door.
Belle is an old-fashioned term for a beautiful woman; 'she was the **belle** of the ball.'

Birth-Berth (See Moor)
Birth is to bring forth new life; to be born, to give **birth** to a baby. (See Born)
Berth is a bunk in a ship; it also refers to ships when they anchor at a wharf; to moor at **berth**.

Bite-Byte-Bight
Bite is to crush, break, cut, or grip with the teeth tightly; to **bite** an apple, to **bite** food.
Byte is a group of bits in a computer.
Bight is a bend in the coastline or shore that opens out into a bay.
Bight is a loose loop in ropes.

Bizarre-Bazaar
Bizarre means strange, extravagant, odd, and eccentric. Not of the norm.
Bazaar is the term used for a market it is a name that comes from the Middle East; it is a place where goods are sold from stalls.

Blue-Blew

Blue is a colour. It is one of the primary colours which are red, green, and **blue**.

Blew is to have blown. 'She **blew** on her soup to cool it down: the wind **blew** the hat off his head.'

Block-Bloc

Block is a solid mass as in a **block** of wood or a **block** of stone.

Block means to obstruct.

Block is a group of flats or apartments: an apartment **block**.

Bloc is a group or combination of people or countries that come together for the same common purpose and beliefs.

Boar-Bore-Boor

Boar is a wild pig with large tusks; wild **boars** are usually found in hot countries such as India and are now being re-introduced back into Britain.

Bore a dull, unexciting, monotonous, repetitive person or situation. (see Bored).

Bore is to drill; 'I need to **bore** a hole in the wall to hang the picture up.'

Boor is a rude person with no manners, usually described as **boor**ish.

Board-Bored (See boarder)

Board is a flat thin piece of stiff wood or card**board**.

Board is to live as a lodger; to rent a room in a house; to receive **board** and lodgings.

Board is to go onto a ship; to climb on **board**.

Board is a committee of people. A committee **board**.

Bored is to feel boredom, to have no mental stimulation, to feel wearisome.

Bored is to have made a hole using a tool such as a drill; he **bored** a hole in the wall.

Boarder-Border (See board).

Boarder is a person that lives in lodgings; it is also a pupil that lives at boarding school

Border is the edge, a boundary, a perimeter.

Border is the dividing line between countries.

Border is the edging around a garden.

Bold-Bowled

Bold means to be fearless, brave, to have courage. (See Bolder)

Bowled is to have played a game of bowls, to have rolled or thrown a ball in bowling.

Bolder-Boulder

Bolder means to be more courageous and braver.

Boulder is a large rock or stone. **Boulder's** are known to break off from mountainsides and roll down to the ground below.

Born-Borne (See Birth)
Born is to have given birth, to have brought forth. The baby was **born** today.
Borne is to have supported, carried, and bore: 'I have **borne** my burdens bravely and endured great suffering.'

Boy-Buoy
Boy is a male child.
Buoy is a floating marker in the sea to warn ships of rocks and other hazards.

Braid-Brayed
Braid is to interweave three or more strands of hair, silk or cotton to form a plait.
Brayed is the loud cry from a donkey; 'the donkey **Brayed** loudly.'

Bread-Bred (See Dough).
Bread is a food made from flour, water and yeast and baked to form a loaf of **bread**.
Bred is to have produced; I **bred** a litter of pedigree puppies. The present tense is to breed.

Brake-Break
Brake is a device or mechanism to slow down or stop a vehicle or bike; to apply the **brakes**.
Break is to shatter, fall to pieces or damage.

Breach-Breech
Breach is to disregard a legal duty, to violate the law, to break an obligation.
Breech is the position of a baby who is feet down instead of head down in the womb. A **breech** birth is where the baby's feet are delivered first.

Brewed-Brood
Brewed is to have boiled, fermented, or infused ingredients to produce a drink. 'I **brewed** a pot of tea: I **brewed** the malt and hops in water to make beer.'
Brood are all the children in one family.
Brood are the young chicks in a family of birds; a **brood** of chicks.
Brood means to be in deep thought; to dwell on something.

Bridal-Bridle
Bridal is to do with weddings, as in **bridal** dress and **bridal** wear.
Bridle is a horse's headgear of which reins are a part of.

Brooch-Broach
Brooch is a piece of jewellery with a pin fastening on the back and worn on clothing.
Broach is to approach a subject, to open a discussion.

Build-Billed
Build is to construct or erect material to form a structure: to **build** a house.
Billed is to be charged a fee for services; to be given a service charge; to be **billed** at a restaurant for a meal.

By-Buy-Bye

By is to be near, as in close **by**.

Buy is to purchase goods, to exchange money for an item or items. I went to the shop to **buy** some sausages.

Bye is short for good**bye**.

Bye is a term used in cricket.

C

Callous-Callus

Callous means hard hearted, to feel no sympathy, emotion or compassion for others; to be emotionally hard. To lack feeling.

Callus is a thickening or hardening of the skin.

Canvas-Canvass

Canvas is a strong material made from hemp and used to make tents, sails and the surface for painting on.

Canvass is to campaign and request political support: to ask people to vote for you.

Canon-Cannon

Canon is a priest of the cathedral clergy, a member of the religious order of the church.

Cannon is a large heavy artillery gun that was used in warfare.

Capital-Capitol

Capital refers to a chief city of a country. London is the **capital** city of England; Washington DC is the **capital** city of America.

Capital letters are large letters or upper case letters at the beginning of a sentence or a name of a person or country; **capital** letters, A B C as opposed to small letters, or lower case letters, a, b, c.

Capitol refers to America's government building, the House of Congress on **Capitol** Hill, in Washington DC, America.

Carat-Caret-Carrot-Karat

Carat is a unit of weight for gemstones such as diamonds.

Caret is a spacing symbol or character, shaped like a wedge or inverted V shape.

Carrot is an orange coloured root vegetable.

Karat is the measure of how pure gold is. 24 **karats** is the purest gold.

Cast-Caste

Cast is to throw, chuck, launch, or hurl an object.

Caste is a social class system in India.

Cede-Seed (See Seed)
Cede is to give in, to yield, to surrender.
Seed is the germinated part of a plant that vegetation grows from, such as plant **seeds**, crop **seeds**, grass **seeds** and the pip or a stone contained within fruit.
Seed is a top tennis player.

Ceiling -Sealing
Ceiling is the overhead upper part of a room.
Sealing is securing and closing something tightly, to make air tight, water proof, and safe proof, as in **sealing** an envelope.

Cell-Sell
Cell is a small room such as a prison **cell**.
Cell is found in the blood, and is called a Blood **Cell**.
Sell is to exchange goods for money.

Cellar-Seller
Cellar is the lowest room in the house; the basement.
Seller is someone who sells goods in exchange for money, such as a market **seller**.

Censer-Censor-Sensor
Censer is a container that is used to burn incense in.
Censor is an official person that examines, reads, or watches, books, films or programmes to ban anything that is offensive and objectionable.
Sensor is an instrument or device that detects or receives a stimulus such as, motion, light, heat or pressure and responds to it.

Census-Senses
Census is an official periodic count of a population.
Senses refers to the five **senses**, hearing, sight, taste, smell and touch.
Senses refers to a perception of something, such as a feeling; 'he **senses** something exciting is about to happen.'

Cent-Scent-Sent (See cents)
Cent is part of the United States currency, a coin used in America; it is 100th part of a dollar.
Scent is perfume, a fragrance, an odour, an aroma, a certain smell. (See scents).
Sent is to have dispatched, issued and transmitted; to have directed to a certain location; the letter was **sent** yesterday: the troops have been **sent** out.

Cents-Sense (See cent)

Cents are American coins; 100 **cents** make a dollar.

Sense refers to either one of the five senses hearing, sight, taste, smell or touch; 'you have a good **sense** of smell'. (see Senses)

Sense refers to 'good practical judgement or common **sense**:' to make **sense** of something.

Cereal-Serial

Cereal is made from grains, such as, oats, maize, wheat, barley and rye which are used to make breakfast food such as Porridge oats.

Serial is something presented in instalments; it is a series of things.

Chance-Chants

Chance is the probability of something occurring or not occurring, a happening not planned; 'It happened by **chance**: **chance** is it may never happen: I'll take a **chance**.'

Chants are to sing or shout words in a repetitive manner.

Chants are songs sung at football matches by the fans.

Chants are short religious songs or psalms, sung on one note with a simple melody.

Chard-Charred

Chard is a leafy green vegetable.

Charred means to blacken by burning.

Chased-Chaste

Chased is to have ran, followed, or pursued someone or something, or to be pursued, followed, hunted, or ran after.

Chaste is to be pure, virginal, innocent, free from temptation.

Check-Cheque

Check is to inspect, examine; to investigate, to look over something to make sure it is correct and in **check**.

Check is a pattern of squares and lines.

Cheque is a money order instructing a bank to pay out a certain amount of cash. It is a small form on which is written the name of the receiver and the amount to be paid.

Chile-Chilli-Chilly

Chile is a country in South America.

Chilli is a hot pepper usually the capsicum pepper.

Chilly means to feel cold, to feel **chilly**.

Chute-Shoot

Chute is a sloping channel or tunnel on which things slide down. The slippery part of a slide is called a **chute**.

Shoot is to expel something at force such as a bow from an arrow or a bullet from a gun.

Choose-Chews

Choose is to select, to pick out or to decide; 'I **choose** to buy this book instead of the other book.'

Chews is grinding, or crushing with the teeth, (masticating.)

Choux-Shoe-Shoo

Choux is a light pastry used in making chocolate éclairs and chocolate profiterole buns.

Shoe is a footwear worn on the foot.

Shoo is to chase away someone or something.

Cite-Sight-Site

Cite is to quote from a book.

Cite is to refer to an author, passage or book.

Cite is to call upon someone to officially appear in court.

Sight is to see and to have vision: it's the ability of seeing. (see and seen)

Site is a place or a location. A building **site**.

Claws-Clause

Claws are sharp curved nails on an animals' paws.

Clause is usually a stipulation or condition in a contract.

Click-Clique

Click is a short sharp sound: a **click** of the fingers.

Click into place is a term used when something fits together or when something makes sense.

Clique is an exclusive or a tight knit group who share the same things in common and who are not open to other people joining their circle.

Close-Clothes

Close is to shut something; '**close** the door; **close** the window; **close** the book.'

Clothes are what we wear on our bodies; trousers, jeans, dresses, Jumpers, socks.

Coarse-Course

Coarse means harsh, rough, and not smooth, such as sand paper or a nail file.

Coarse means vulgar, offensive, or crude language, behaviour or manners.

Course refers to a particular path or direction followed to get to a destination.

Course is a series of things, such as a **course** of treatment or a **course** of medication.

Course refers to a number of meals at one sitting. A starter, a main meal and a dessert is called a three **course** dinner.

Course is the study of a series of subjects or lessons in a particular area of learning; 'I am studying a **course** in biology.'

Coat-Cote

Coat is an outer garment worn to keep us warm when the weather is cold; **coat**s come in various lengths, colours and styles.

Cote is a shed, a pen, or a coop where smaller animals are housed.

Coax-Cokes

Coax is to persuade or to gently influence a person.

Cokes are fizzy soda pop drinks.

Colonel-Kernel

Colonel is an officer in the air force, army and navy, it is the rank below a brigadier general but higher than a lieutenant.

Kernel is the inner part of a nut or fruit; it is the central core.

Comments-Commence

Comments are remarks, observations, opinions, explanations.

Commence means to start, to proceed, to initiate, to begin, to carry on.

Complacent-Complaisant

Complacent is to be self-satisfied with not trying harder, it is to have no desire to do more than you have to.

Complaisant is to fit in with others, a willingness to please, to be agreeable.

Complement-Compliment

Complement means to suit, to match, to make whole, to complete the finishing touch; 'it's the full **complement**.'

Compliment is to flatter, admire, appreciate, or give praise; 'your new hairstyle looks lovely.'

Confidant-Confident

Confidant is someone that secrets are entrusted to.

Confident is to be self assured and to have self belief. To be **confident** is to have faith, to have total trust.

Cops-Copse

Cops is slang for police, it is a term generally used in America.

Copse is a dense area containing a thicket of shrubs or trees.

Cord-Chord-Cored

Cord is a long piece of string, rope or flex of wire.

Chord is a group of musical notes played in harmony to make a tune.

Cored is to have removed the central part of something, such as an apple.

Coo-Coup

Coo is the sound that Doves make.

Coup is an attack to take over government power usually by an army.

Correspondents-Correspondence
Correspondents are people that keep in communication with others and pass on information, they keep us up to date and informed. A news reporter, a journalist, is a **correspondent**.
Correspondence means similarity, likeness, and suitability, for example, 'the results of the two laboratory tests are in **correspondence** with each other, they are similar.'

Council-Counsel
Council is a collective group that govern a city or town, give advice and deal with administration; Borough councils look after housing needs and County **councils** look after the running of their local cities and towns. (See Councillor)
Counsel is to give advice, to consult with, to entrust with secrets. (See Counsellor)

Councillor-Counsellor
Councillor is a member of a collective group, (see council).
Counsellor is one who advices. (see Counsel)

Craft-Kraft
Craft means skill, ability, talent; someone that is skilled in a trade. 'His **craft** is Carpentry.'
Kraft is a paper bag or wrapping paper made of wood pulp.

Creak-Creek
Creak is to make a squeaking, and/or grating noise, for example when walking on a squeaky floorboard.
Creek is an expanse of water, smaller than a river; a stream.

Crewel-Cruel
Crewel is a piece of worsted yarn that is used for embroidery.
Cruel is to deliberately harm, inflict physical, verbal or emotional pain and suffering on another person or animal.

Cue-Queue
Cue is a stick used to play snooker or pool with, it is used to hit the balls.
Cue is a signal to begin, start or commence; 'when I give you the **cue** (signal) you may then begin.'
Queue is a line of people waiting to be served in a shop or waiting to get on a bus. It is forming an orderly line and waiting your turn.

Cygnet-Signet
Cygnet is a young swan.
Signet was a mark used in the past to authenticate documents.
Signet is a ring that is worn on the finger; a **signet** ring.

Currant-Current
Currant is a fruit; it is a small berry such as a raisin.
Current refers to contemporary, up to date, the present time, such as 'the **current** trend is to wear silver jewellery.'
Current is the movement of water in one direction.

Cymbal-Symbol
Cymbal is a musical instrument usually made of brass and round in shape; two **cymbals** are used to bang together to produce a loud clanging sound.
Symbol is a representation of something such as a sign, emblem, image or logo.

D
Days-Daze
Days refers to the **days** of the week, Monday, Tuesday, Wednesday, Thursday, Friday, Saturday and Sunday. There are seven **days** in a week.
Daze is to stun and/or shock; he banged his head hard and was in a **daze**.
Daze is surprise or wonderment; 'I bumped into a handsome and famous actor unexpectedly and was in a **daze** for days.'

Descent-Decent- Dissent
Descent is to go down, as in going down the stairs; a downward decline.
Descent refers to family heritage, lineage, and ancestry.
Decent means respectable, good, or well behaved.
Decent is a word used when referring to someone's kind behaviour; 'it was **decent** of him to lend me his coat when I was cold.'
Dissent is to disagree.

Dew-Due
Dew are drops of moisture that form when the air cools; they are seen on grass and plants early in the morning and are called **dew** drops.
Due is when something is owed or expected; 'my phone bill is now **due**: my sister's baby is **due** next week.'

Dear-Deer
Dear is a term of endearment. 'Hello my **dear**, how are you.'
Dear refers to something that is high in price and expensive to buy.
Deer is an animal that lives amongst woodlands; they are rein**deer** with the males having large antlers.

Discreet-Discrete
Discreet is to be prudent, careful, diplomatic, and tactful.
Discrete means separate parts, as in 'two **discrete** parts.'

Discussed-Disgust

Discussed is to have debated, to have talked it over, to have had interesting conversation.

Disgust is to be repulsed, revolted and to have a deep dislike for something.

Diverse-Divers

Diverse is to be different, to be unlike others or other things.

Divers are people whose job it is to dive underwater searching for things.

Divers are people that dive for sports and compete in competitions.

Divers are large birds that dive underwater for food.

Doc-Dock

Doc is the shortened term for **doc**tor.

Dock is where ships sail into to unload cargo, load cargo, or to be repaired; it is a waterway, a port.

Dock is a name for the enclosure that prisoners usually stand in when appearing in court.

Dock is a large leafed, dark green weed called a **Dock** weed. These large green leaves were used to rub on stings when stung by a stinging nettle to ease the pain.

Doe-Dough

Doe is a female deer, rabbit, or hare.

Dough is a thick mixture of flour, water and other mixtures that are used to bake bread. (See bread).

Done-Dun

Done means to have carried something out and completed it, 'I have **done** the washing up.'

Dun is to demand a payment of money.

Dual-Duel

Dual means two elements or two parts as in a '**dual** carriageway.'

Duel is an arranged fight between two people using weapons to settle an argument or disagreement.

Die-Dye

Die is to cease to live and exist, it is being dead, an end to something, to be deceased.

Dye is a colour or stain, it is used to colour such things as materials and hair.

Dire-Dyer

Dire is when something is awful, urgent and dreadful; 'I am in **dire** need of help; this is a **dire** situation.'

Dyer is someone that colours something to change its natural colour; the dress was yellow but the **dyer** dyed it pink.

Draft-Draught

Draft is a sketch of an idea, a preliminary drawing of a rough plan.
Draught is a current of cold air.
Draught is a measure of drink, usually alcohol.

Dyeing-Dying (See Dye, Die, Dyer)

Dyeing is applying colour to something: 'I am **dyeing** my white T-shirt pink.'
Dying is gradually passing away, weakening, perishing; it is on the way to being deceased, dead.

E

Earn-Erne-Urn

Earn is to receive payment for work done, to **earn** the fruits of labour, to receive what is deserved.
Erne is a sea eagle.
Urn is a vase that is used to put the ashes of deceased persons in that have been cremated.
Urn is a large metal container used for making tea or coffee.

Edition-Addition

Edition is the number of times a copy is published, such as a book.
Addition is anything that is added, or has something added onto or into it: an additive.

Effect-Affect

Effect is the result of a cause or an outcome: to carry out something creates an **effect**: 'I decorated my bedroom in lilac and the **effect** was amazing.'
Affect means to move the emotions; 'his singing had such an **affect** on me that I was moved to tears.'

Elicit-Illicit

Elicit is to evoke something, to bring it forth; 'I asked her a question to **elicit** a response.'
Illicit is unlawful, illegal.

Elude-Allude

Elude means to escape, flee, avoid, evade.
Allude means to hint at or refer to something.

Elusion-Illusion

Elusion is evading, hard to find.
Illusion is a fantasy, a figment of the imagination. An **Illusion** is used in conjuring tricks.

Elusive-Illusive

Elusive means hard to find, evasive, slippery.
Illusive is to mislead, to have false hope, a sham, unreal.

Emerge-Immerge
Emerge is to come forth, to come into view, to come to light.
Immerge is to submerge into water; 'when I dive I **immerge** into the water.'

Ensure-Insure
Ensure is to make sure, to make certain, to make secure.
Insure is to guarantee against damage, loss, harm or death, usually on businesses, homes, cars and people; to take out an insurance policy.

Essay-Assay
Essay is a written piece of work, which is on a particular subject that students study at schools, colleges and universities. It is part of the coursework.
Assay is to test, examine and analyse metals such as gold and silver which is tested for quality.

Ewe-Yew-You
Ewe is a female sheep.
Yew is a tree.
You refers to one or more person or persons; 'I love **you**: **you** did well: are **you** all going to the party tomorrow? All of **you** passed your exams.'

Except-Accept
Except means to omit, exclude or leave out; 'we can all go to the beach **except** Tim because he has to work today.'
Accept is to agree to something; 'I **accept** that what you have told me is true.'
Accept is to acquire and obtain; 'thank you, I **accept** this award: I **accept** your apology.'

Exercise-Exorcise
Exercise is physical or mental activity.
Exorcise is to expel evil spirits through prayers.

Eye-Aye-I (See Aye and I)
Eye is an organ of sight, which we see from.
Eye is the hole in a needle that the cotton threads through.
Aye is a dialect for yes, '**aye**, I agree.' It is usually a dialect spoken in the north of England and Scotland.
Aye aye captain is a response given to an order, **aye** captain is in agreement in naval language.
I refers to oneself, 'me myself and **I**.'

Eyelet-Islet (See Isle)
Eyelet is the hole made in fabric to place hooks or cords through.
Islet is a small Island.

F

Facts-Fax

Facts are actualities, evidence that show something exists and is right, the truth.

Fax is a machine that duplicates and sends printed information electronically to another **fax** machine.

Fain-Feign

Fain is to be willing, happy to oblige, ready and eager.

Feign is to pretend, to act falsely, giving a false impression, to act showy or to make excuses.

Faint-Feint

Faint is to pass out and lose consciousness. To feel **faint** is to feel lightheaded, dizzy and giddy.

Faint means dim, lacking clarity, not clear; 'through the fog I saw a **faint** figure: my printer is running out of ink and the words are coming out **faint**.'

Feint is to pretend, to deceive, to imagine and to trick; to draw attention away from the real intention. The boxer made a **feint** (pretended) he was going to hit with his right hand but used his left hand instead.

Fair-Fare

Fair is to be unbiased, unprejudiced, open minded. To make **fair** decisions.

Fair is to have blonde hair, to be light coloured.

Fair describes the weather when it is dry and warm.

Fair is a fete. A travelling **fair** is one that stops at different locations around the country setting up amusement rides called a **fair** ground. (See Fete)

Fare means a fee, a price, the cost of travelling on a bus, train, boat, or plane.

Fate-Fete

Fate refers to destiny and the predetermined forces that map out events.

Fete is another name for a travelling fair. (see Fair).

Father-Farther

Father is a male parent, one who exercises paternal care over his children.

Father refers to fore **fathers**, past ancestors, the founder of a family blood line. (See Descent).

Farther means, far away, not close by, not near here; 'the next town is **farther** away than we realised and it is of a greater distance.'

Faze-Phase

Faze is to make someone feel uneasy, flustered, agitated or uncomfortable in themselves by another person's behaviour or actions.

Phase refers to a process, a change, a season, a stage or a sequence; 'sucking his thumb is just a **phase** he is going through: the moon is in its quarterly **phase**.'

Feet-Feat

Feet have toes attached and are the lower limbs below the ankles which we walk on.
Feet is the old measure of unit; feet and inches.
Feat refers to a daring display of boldness and skill, an achievement; 'the stunt bike rider performed an amazing **feat** by jumping over twenty cars.'

Few-Phew

Few means not many, less of, not a lot.
Phew is a noise made when expressing relief or disgust at something.

File-Phial (See Phial)

File is a tool or implement with a coarse surface used for smoothing or shaping rough edges.
File is an orderly queue or single line where people stand behind each other.
File is a recording of related information or data which is kept on **file**.
File is a box or folder in which papers are kept in a particular order.
Phial is a small glass cylindrical bottle used for storing liquids. (See Vial)

Find-Fined

Find is to discover something or to recover something that is lost.
Fined is to have a financial penalty or punishment imposed.

Finish-Finnish

Finish is to terminate, to come to an end, to complete or close something.
Finnish refers to someone who is from the country Finland.

Fir-Fur

Fir is a tree, 'the **fir** tree,' it has pine needles and cones.
Fur is the coat of an animal such as the beaver, fox and leopard.

Flare-Flair

Flare is to burst forth as in a bright light or a flame of fire.
Flare is the widening of nostrils; When she gets angry her nostrils **flare**.
Flare is the wide width of trousers at the ankle.
Flair is to have a natural skill, talent or ability; a **flair** for certain things: 'Shakespeare had a natural **flair** for writing plays.'

Flaw-Floor

Flaw means imperfection, defect, fault; 'I bought a book and it had a **flaw** where the page was missing some words.'
Floor is the surface of a room or hallway on which we walk.

Flee-Flea

Flee is to escape, to run away from something threatening.

Flea is a small jumping insect without wings that feeds off the blood of warm-blooded mammals.

Flecks-Flex

Flecks are small particles of colour or light.

Flex is an insulated electrical cord.

Flex means to bend the arm, knee or part of the body. **Flex** is to stretch and contract the muscles.

Flew-Flue-Flu

Flew is the past of fly. The bird **flew** past my window.

Flue is a tube type chute in which chimney smoke, gasses and fumes pass up through into the air.

Flu is short for influenza, a contagious virus.

Flower-Flour

Flower is the part of a plant that produces petals to form a bloom such as a daisy, rose or chrysanthemum.

Flour is ground grain formed to a soft fine powder which is used in baking.

Foe-Faux

Foe means enemy.

Faux means artificial, an imitation, not real, false.

For-Four-Fore

For is used in the context of a function word, in support or favour of, on behalf of, in defence and direction of: 'for example: I did it **for** you: the flowers are **for** my mum: I am voting **for** the other team: they're not **for** you: I acted **for** the best: go **for** it.'

Four is the number after three and the number before five; three, **four**, five. (See fourth)

Fore means at the front; 'it is at the **fore** front of cutting edge technology.'

Forgo-Forego

Forgo means to abstain, to pass up something, to go without.

Forego is to go before, to precede.

Formally-Formerly

Formally refers to procedures carried out in the correct and conventional manner that is customary; 'the fete was **formally** opened by the mayor.'

Formerly means at a time previously in the past; '**formerly** this village did not have a railway station, but it does now.'

Foreword-Forward

Foreword is an introduction about a book, it is usually written by someone else other than the author.

Forward is to go forth, to move toward the direction one is facing; to be further ahead or advanced. The opposite of backwards.

Foul-Fowl

Foul means disgusting, unpleasant, filthy, rude, repulsive, or stinking; the contents of the dustbin smell and look **foul**: that person's rude behaviour is **foul**.

Foul is a term used in sport when the rules are broken.

Fowl are chickens, ducks and turkeys, which are used for their eggs and meat; there are also wild **fowl** such as water**fowl** and geese.

Fourth-Forth

Fourth comes after third and before fifth, **fourth** refers to number four, he came in at **fourth** place. (See Four)

Forth is to go forward, to head onwards: the rock climber ventured **forth** up the mountain: she paced the room back and **forth**: the man in the crowd came **forth** and asked for the actor's autograph.

Frees-Freeze-Frieze

Frees is to release, to not be obligated, to be free from confinement.

Freeze is to turn liquid to ice or to preserve food by storing it in extremely cold temperatures such as a freezer.

Frieze is a long band of decorated or sculpted wall art.

G

Gate-Gait

Gate is an entrance or exit on hinges usually within a wall, fence or hedge and made of metal or wood

Gait is a way of walking; it is the manner in which a person moves.

Genes-Jeans

Genes are carried within the chromosomes and make up our DNA; they determine what we will look like.

Jeans are trousers made from denim material.

Gilt-Guilt

Gilt is a thin overlay of gold paint or gold leaf applied to a surface.

Guilt is a feeling of remorse or self-reproach in having done something wrong.

Gnu-Knew-New (See Knew)

Gnu is a large South African antelope.

Knew is to have gained knowledge and information, to have perceived, to have remembered and understood; to have known; 'I **knew** it was your birthday because I remembered.'

New is fresh, not used before, recently made, contemporary, current; 'I have just bought a **new** pair of shoes.'

Gorilla-Guerrilla

Gorilla is a very large ape of central Africa.

Guerrilla is a member of a small independent fighting force.

Grate-Great

Grate is to grind, scrape, shred, or rub. To **grate** cheese: to **grate** the teeth together.

Grate is a word used to express annoyance or irritation with someone; 'they **grate** on my nerves.'

Grate is the metal frame in a fireplace that holds fuel, such as coal.

Great means big, large, numerous and immense: of a **great** size: 'a **great** many were present at the conference on wildlife.'

Great refers to something good; 'I had a **great** time on my birthday.'

Great is used to describe something or someone of importance: 'Einstein was a man of **great** intelligence: my **great** grandmother is 100 years old.'

Grease-Greece

Grease is a thick oily substance that has many uses. It is used to lubricate with, to cook with and for cosmetic purposes for moisturising or protecting the skin.

Greece is a country in Europe and is on the border with Turkey.

Grill-Grille

Grill is metal bars (found in an oven or cooker), used to conduct heat downwards to cook food. To **grill** food.

Grille are metal bars, grating, or wire, used as a screen to protect or separate something.

Groan-Grown

Groan is to utter a deep mournful sound of annoyance, pain, sadness or disapproval.

Groan is a sound made under pressure when something too heavy in weight is applied.

Grown is to have matured, reached adult hood, became taller, expanded or increased in size.

Guest-Guessed

Guest is a visitor, a caller, someone who is shown hospitality; a hotel **guest**, a party **guest**, a wedding **guest**. Someone invited to a social gathering or invited to someone's home.

Guessed is to have predicted or made an assumption, to have formed an opinion based on reasoning; 'I **guessed** she would buy that dress.'

Gym-Jim

Gym is a shortened word for **gym**nasium. It is a place where physical exercise is carried out.
Jim is a man's name, usually short for **Jim**my and the nickname for James.

H

Hair-Hare-Herr

Hair is the thread like strands that grow on the scalp and skin of humans and animals.
Hare is a long eared mammal that lives in fields; it is a cousin of the rabbit but larger in size.
Herr is the German word for Mr.

Hale-hail

Hale means healthy, free from sickness; 'hale and hearty.'
Hail is the ice pellets that rain down in stormy weather.
Hail is to salute and to greet with respect; the roman emperors were hailed, for example 'hail Caesar.'

Hall-Haul

Hall is an entrance, a corridor, a large room, an assembly room or a passageway in a house.
Haul is to carry, pull, tug or drag something.
Haul is the long distance when travelling; 'it is a long **haul** from London to Scotland.'

Hanger-Hangar

Hangar is a large storage area used for storing aeroplanes in.
Hanger is used for hanging clothes on; it is made out of wood, plastic, or metal with a hook at the top for hanging onto a clothes rail.

Heard-Herd

Heard is to have perceived sound, to have listened; 'I **heard** the doorbell ring: I **heard** what you said.' (See hear)
Herd is a number of animals in a group; a **herd** of cows, a **herd** of elephants.

Heart-Hart

Heart is the large organ that pumps blood around the body.
Hart is a male deer from the red deer family.

Heed-He'd

Heed is to pay careful attention to, to take notice of.
He'd is a contraction or a shortened word for 'he had or he would.'

Heel-Heal-He'll

Heel is the back part of the foot under the ankle.
Heal is to become well, to mend, to recover from an illness or injury.
He'll is a contraction or a shortened word for 'he will'.

Heir-Air (See air)

Heir is a relative or a person entitled to inherit goods or money that a deceased person has left to them.

Air is the atmosphere surrounding us that we breathe.

Here-Hear

Here refers to this place at this time; 'we are **here**: put the vase of flowers **here**: **here** is the book: **here** we are.'

Hear is to listen to, to perceive sounds; 'I can **hear** the birds singing.' (See heard)

Heroin-Heroine

Heroin is a narcotic drug derived from morphine and is highly addictive.

Heroine is a woman of courage and great deeds, it is also the leading female character in a book, film or play.

Hi-High

Hi is an expression of saying hello, it is a short form of greeting someone.

High is a great height, it means tall, elevated or towering above; 'the plane flew **high** in the sky.'

Higher-Hire

Higher is taller, loftier, above, overhead.

Hire is to engage the service of someone or something for a period of time, for a payment or a fee.

Hoard-Horde

Hoard is a collection, preservation, or storage of food or items for future use.

Horde is a large group or a crowd of people.

Hoarse-Horse

Hoarse refers to a gruff voice, a gravely, rough and throaty sound when speaking.

Horse is a large four-footed hoofed animal, used for riding on or for pulling carts.

Hole-Whole (See Whole)

Hole is a cavity, an aperture, a gap, a hollow area.; 'my sock has a **hole** in it.' (See holey)

Whole means, complete, total, the **whole** number, the full amount and quantity. 'I now have the **whole** amount of money to buy a new bike.'

Holey-Holy-Wholly

Holey is something that has a hole or holes in it. (See Hole)

Holy is sacred, saintly, sinless, righteous and belonging to God.

Wholly is the whole amount.

Hoes-Hose
Hoes are long handled garden tools with a flat blade used for digging out weeds.
Hose is a long thin tube in which liquid passes through; a garden **hose** is used for watering plants.

Hour-Our
Hour is time and has 60 minutes in it. (See hours)
Our is associated with and belonging to us: 'it is **our** home.' (See ours)

Hours-Ours (See hour and our)
Hours refers to time, there are 24 **hours** in a day. **Hours** refers to more than one hour: 'we waited at the airport for **hours**: the party is **hours** away yet.'
Ours means something belonging to us, 'it is **ours**.'

Humerus-Humorous
Humerus is the long arm bone between the shoulder and the elbow.
Humorous is something funny, comical and amusing.

Hymn-Him
Hymn is a song of praise and worship, sung to God usually in churches.
Him refers to the male; a boy or a man: 'it's **him**: I saw **him** the other day.'

I

I-Aye-Eye (See Aye and Eye)
I refers to oneself, 'me myself and **I**.'
Aye is a dialect for yes; '**aye** I agree.'
Aye aye captain is a response given to an order, **aye** captain is in agreement in naval language.
Eye is an organ of sight, which we see from.
Eye is the hole in a needle that the cotton threads through.

Idle-Idol
Idle is to be lazy, inactive, not doing anything, not in use.
Idol is an image of a deity that is worshipped.

I'll-Isle-Aisle (See Aisle)
I'll is a contraction; it is a shorter way of saying 'I will.' '**I'll** be straight back.'
Isle means Island. An island is land that is surrounded by water. The **Isle** of white. Britain is an island, the British **Isles**. (See Island and Eyelet)
Aisle is the gangway or walkway between a row of seats in a church; 'the bride looked lovely as she walked down the **aisle**.'

In-Inn

In is to be inside, enclosed within, or belonging to something. 'Will you be **in** this afternoon: she is **in** the Army: it belongs **in** there.'

Inn is an establishment that offers lodging, food and drink for the traveller, such as a motel or hotel.

Incite-Insight

Incite is to rouse, excite, spur on, provoke, goad; to motivate someone or a crowd into action.

Insight is to have perception, understanding, awareness and intuition; the ability to be able to discern.

Ireland-Island

Ireland is a country consisting of northern and southern **Ireland** with Dublin being the capital.

Ireland is known as the emerald isle because of its rich green lands.

Island is the land that is surrounded by water. (See Isle and Eyelet).

Islet-Eyelet

Islet is a small Island. (See Isle and Island)

Eyelet is a hole made in fabric to place hooks or cords through.

J

Jam-Jamb

Jam is a conserve made from fruit and boiled with sugar to make a thick sweet mixture such as strawberry **Jam**.

Jam means to become wedged between something, to become stuck.

Jam is to pack tightly or squeeze into a small or limited amount of space.

Jam is to push something with force; '**Jam** it into that hole.'

Jamb is the sidepieces that form the frames to doors, windows, arches and fireplaces.

Juggler-Jugular

Juggler is someone that continuously throws and keeps more than one object in the air and catches them as they fall.

Jugular refers to the throat or the neck.

K

Key-Quay

Key is a metal implement shaped to fit exactly into keyholes to lock and unlock doors, boxes and safes.

Key is a musical note and pitch.

Key is an Island or reef, usually in the Caribbean.

Key refers to something of importance or significance.

Quay is the place ships dock to have their cargo loaded or unloaded.

Knead-Need
Knead is to press and squeeze dough mixture into a pliable form.
Need is a requirement, a necessity, something that is wanted.

Knew-New-Gnu (see Gnu)
Knew is to have gained knowledge and information, to have perceived, to have understood and remembered: 'I **knew** it was your birthday: I already **knew** a lot about the subject on fishing.'
New is fresh, not used before, recently made, contemporary, current: 'I have just bought a **new** pair of shoes.'
Gnu is a large South African antelope.

Knit-Nit
Knit is to form loops with wool and knitting needles, which are intertwined and made into a garment such as a jumper or cardigan. Glenda decided to **knit** a cardigan.
Nit is the egg of the louse that lives in the hair, they are called head lice.

Knight-Night
Knight was a medieval soldier in the middle ages, they wore steel armour for protection.
Knight is a title of honour given by a sovereign head such as the queen who can bestow **knight**hoods.
Night refers to **night**-time, when the day has ended and it is dark outside.

Know-No
Know is to understand the facts, to have knowledge, perception and information. Past tense is known and knew. (See knew)
No is generally used as a negative connotation, as a refusal, or to deny: '**no** I cannot meet you: **no** you cannot come with me: the answer to your question is **no**.' It can also be used in the positive, '**no** you are not to blame.'

Knows-Nose
Knows is to have gained knowledge or information. It is to understand, to memorize, or be aware of something; 'he **knows** how to fix the car: she **knows** alot about wildlife.'
Nose is the organ of smell in the middle of the face.

Knot-Not
Knot is a twisted tangle in a loop of a piece of string, neck-chain or rope.
knot is found in the wood of trees.
Knot is the speed at which a ship travels.
Not is used mainly in the negative; 'it is **not** for you: you cannot have the day off.' It can also be used in the positive, 'the worst possible scenario is **not** going to happen: you are **not** going to lose your job.'

L

Lathe-Lath

Lathe is a machine that is used to shape metal and wood.
Lath is a narrow strip of wood of which several pieces are used to make a trellis with.

Lacks-Lax

Lacks is something that is needed or missing; 'this food **lacks** flavour'.
Lax is loose, relaxed, slack.'

Law-Lore

Law is a set of rules and regulations with penalties imposed by an authority or governing body.
Lore is knowledge or teaching of a particular subject. 'The **lore** of Mathematics.'

Leak-Leek

Leak is a loss of liquid, air or gas escaping through a hole or a crack.
Leek is a vegetable belonging to the onion and garlic family.

Lean-Lien

Lean means to bend to one side, recline, slant, slope and incline.
Lean refers to meat that has no fat on it.
Lien is to secure your property against a loan until the loan is paid back.

Least-Leased

Least means less of something, not as much, of the smallest amount or importance.
Leased is to have rented out property or land for a contracted time in return for payment.

Lessen-Lesson

Lessen is to reduce, to become less, to make smaller.
Lesson is part of a series of courses broken down into time slots and usually studied in a classroom.

Levy-Levee

Levy is to impose payment of tax on goods sold.
Levee is an embankment built along rivers or seas to protect against flooding.

Liable-Libel

Liable is to be responsible and legally obliged by law; 'the railway companies are **liable** for ensuring the safety of their passengers.'
Liable means more likely or probable; 'she is **liable** to book a holiday abroad.'
Libel is to write and publish words that are false and/or damaging to another person's reputation.

Liar-Lyre
Liar is someone that does not tell the truth.
Lyre is a small stringed instrument from the harp family, which originates from Greece.

Links-Lynx
Links are the separate round pieces which connect to make a chain. Anything that connects one thing to another.
Lynx is a wildcat.

Lightening-lightning
Lightening is to lighten colour, to make lighter or brighter.
Lightening is to make something less heavy; '**lightening** the load.'
Lightning is the discharge of flash in the sky when there is a thunderstorm.

Loan-Lone
Loan is to lend someone an item or money on the promise that the item is returned or the money paid back.
Lone is to be alone, without company, to be isolated, solitary, to be by oneself.

Loos-Lose
Loos is a common term for toilets.
Lose refers to something going missing, mislaid, not able to retain, not able to find, or fail to win.

Lumbar-Lumber
Lumbar refers to the lower part of the back.
Lumber is timber cut from trees and sawn into boards or planks of wood.
Lumber is to be heavy footed, to move clumsily, to move noisily.
Lumber is to load, to burden, to impose problems or trouble onto another person; 'don't **lumber** me with your problems.'

M
Made-Maid
Made is to have created, prepared, built, designed, completed, and produced something; 'the carpenter **made** these wooden chairs: I **made** that cake.'
Made is to cause something to happen; 'she **made** the promotions: she **made** me smile with her compliment: she **made** it onto the train just in time.'
Maid is a female servant.

Male-Mail

Male refers to men and boys, the **male** species.

Mail are the letters and parcels that are posted and delivered to us.

Mall-Maul

Mall is a shopping centre where many shops are located in one single large building.

Maul is to handle someone roughly, to ferociously attack someone or to be attacked by an animal.

Mane-Main

Mane is the hair that grows around the back and neck of lions and horses.

Main means the chief principle, something of primary importance: the **main** reason for doing something.

Manner-Manor

Manner is the behaviour of a person; it pertains to their demeanour.

Manner is a customary way of doing things.

Manor is a mansion. It is a large main house with many rooms and is surrounded by land; The Lord and Lady of the **manor** lives there.

Maize-Maze

Maize is a cereal plant; it is also known as corn.

Maze is a confusing network of interconnecting passages or paths usually surrounded by hedges and designed to make it difficult to find the way out.

Martial-Marshall

Martial relates to war and military life.

Marshall is an officer of a high rank in some police forces and armies in countries such as France and America.

Meat-Meet-Mete

Meat is the flesh of animals used as food such as pork, beef, lamb and poultry.

Meet is to encounter, to bump into someone, to arrange to be present at a designated time and place, to be introduced to someone for the first time, to make his or her acquaintance.

Mete is to distribute out, to give out in quantities and portions at a time.

Medal-Meddle

Medal is a star, a cross, or a round circular shape made of metal and usually attached to a ribbon given as an award for an event, bravery, merit, or action: 'my grandfather won a **medal** for his bravery during the war: the Olympic swimmer won a gold **medal** for coming first.'

Meddle is to interfere, to intrude, to involve oneself in other people's affairs uninvited.

Metal-Mettle
Metal is Gold, silver, tin, iron and copper. Zinc and copper are mixed together to make brass.
Mettle means brave, courageous, bold and daring.

Meter-Metre
Meter is an apparatus used for measuring the usage of water, gas, electricity and length of time, as in a parking **meter**.
Metre is a unit of length, replacing the old system of feet and inches.

Might-Mite
Might refers to possibly, perhaps, likelihood, may well. 'I **might** cook tonight but I'm not sure: he **might** change his mind.'
Might refers to strength and power; 'he is full of **might**.'
Mite is a small parasite, a tiny insect.

Mince-Mints
Mince is to cut something up or chop into small pieces such as minced beef.
Mints are herbaceous plants, their leaves are used for their mint flavour in seasoning and cooking food.
Mints are sweets that taste of mint.

Miner-Minor
Miner is someone that works down a mine, such as a coal miner.
Minor is a person under the legal age of adulthood.
Minor refers to something small in size or not as important.

Missed-Mist
Missed is to have failed to hit a target, to not hear something, to not turn up for an appointed date or to forget an event; 'I **missed** her birthday: I **missed** my appointment: I **missed** hitting the ball: I **missed** the deadline: I **missed** what he said because I couldn't hear him.'
Mist is an expanse of water vapour, a cloud of condensation, like a fine fog.

Moan-Mown
Moan is to make a sound of disapproval, of being in pain or to complain.
Mown is to have cut something down; 'the neighbours **mown** grass looks tidy.'

Mode-Mowed
Mode is a certain style, a method or particular way of doing things.
Mode is the current fashion in clothing and art.
Mowed is to have mown, cut down, 'I mowed the grass earlier today.'

Mood-Mooed
Mood is an emotion, a state of mind; 'I feel in a happy **mood**.'
Mooed is the noise a cow made; 'the cow **mooed** loudly.'

More-Moor
More means extra or additional, a larger number, amount, or quantity, or to a greater degree or extent.
Moor is an expanse of peat wasteland which is often marshy and covered by the heather plant.
Moor is securing a ship by anchor or cable. (See berth)

Morning-Mourning
Morning is the early part of the day before the afternoon, the start of a new day.
Mourning is weeping, grieving, lamenting, due to a bereavement with the wearing of black clothes as a sign of sorrow.

Moose-Mousse
Moose is a large deer that lives in North America, it is the largest of the deer family.
Mousse is a sweet dessert made from whipped cream and comes in a variety of flavours such as chocolate, strawberry, and vanilla.

Muse-Mews
Muse means to be deep in thought, to meditate or ponder about something.
Muse is a person used for inspiration and creativity in art or fashion.
Mews is a street, lined with dwellings which were originally stables but have since been converted into homes.

Muscle-Mussel
Muscle is an organ in the body that contracts to allow movement.
Mussel is a bivalve mollusc that lives in saltwater or freshwater. They have oblong shells and cling to rocks.

Mustard-Mustered
Mustard is a pungent condiment made from the mustard seed and is eaten with food.
Mustered is to have collected, assembled, gathered, roused, or summoned: 'the troops were **mustered** up for battle: '**he mustered** up the courage to do a bungee jump.'

N
Naval-Navel
Naval relates to the navy and ships.
Navel is the belly button.

Nee-Knee
Nee refers to the maiden name of a woman before she was married.
Knee is the joint in the middle part of the leg between the thigh and the shin. It enables the leg to bend.

Need-Knead (See Knead)
Need is a requirement, a necessity, something that is wanted.
Knead is to press and squeeze dough mixture into a pliable form.

New-Knew-Gnu (See Gnu and Knew)
New is fresh, not used before, recently made, contemporary, current; 'I have just bought a **new** pair of shoes: the brand **new** mobile phone will be in the shops tomorrow.'
Knew is to have gained knowledge and information, to have perceived, to have understood, and remembered: 'I **knew** it was your birthday because I remembered the date.'
Gnu is a large South African antelope.

Night-knight (See Knight)
Night is **night**-time, when the day has ended and it is dark outside.
Knight was a medieval soldier in the middle ages; they wore steel armour for protection.
Knight is a title of honour given by a sovereign head, such as the queen, who can bestow **knight**hoods.

Nit-Knit (See Knit)
Nit is the egg of the louse that usually lives in the hair, they are called head lice.
Knit is to form loops with wool and knitting needles which are intertwined and made into a garment such as a jumper or cardigan.

Nose-Knows (See Knows)
Nose is the organ of smell in the middle of the face.
Knows is to have knowledge or information. It is to understand, to memorize or be aware of something. 'He **knows** how to fix the car.'

Not-Knot (See Knot)
Not is used mainly in the negative; 'he did **not** go to his appointment: the food does **not** taste nice.' It can also be used in the positive: 'the worst possible scenario is **not** going to happen: you are **not** going to lose your job.'
Knot is a tangle, a loop in a piece of string, neck-chain, or rope.
Knot is found in the wood of trees.
Knot is the speed at which a ship travels.

None-Nun

None means, not any, nothing, not one.

Nun is a woman belonging to a religious order, predominantly the Catholic Church, who has taken a vow of poverty, chastity and obedience to serve God.

O

Oar-Ore-Or

Oar is a long pole with a flattened paddle on the end used for rowing boats.

Ore is a rock from which metal can be extracted called iron **ore**.

Or refers to otherwise, either one **or** the other not both. It is a connective word; 'would you prefer a cake **or** a biscuit,' as opposed to, 'would you like a cake and a biscuit.'

Ode-Owed

Ode is a lyrical poem, a poem to be sung which addresses a particular situation, person or subject.

Owed is to indebted to pay back something borrowed.

Oh-Owe

Oh is an expression used in a response to a remark, situation or to show understanding of something.

Owe is to be in debt to someone, to be obligated for something received. (See owed)

One-Won

One is a single number; it comes before the number two.

Won is to have been victorious, to have come first in a competition or a test. to have succeeded or overcome difficulties.

Oracle-Auricle (See Auricle)

Oracle is the word of god, an answer to something asked. To consult the **oracle**.

Auricle is the outer part of the ear.

Ordinance-Ordnance

Ordinance is an official and authorative statute, regulation, law, command, order or rule; 'a public **ordinance** was made against throwing litter on the pavement.'

Ordinance refers to a religious ritual.

Ordnance is the branch of military supplies of weapons, ammunition, and equipment.

Our-Hour (See Hour)

Our is associated with and belonging to us; 'it is **our** home.'

Hour is time and has 60 minutes in it.

Ours-Hours (See Hours)

Ours means something belonging to us; 'it is **ours**.'

Hours refers to time; their are 24 **hours** in a day. More than one hour is many **hours**; 'we waited at the airport for **hours**: the party is **hours** away yet.'

Overate-Overrate

Overate is to have eaten too much.

Overrate is to value too highly, to place too higher importance or esteem on something or someone.

Overdue-Overdo

Overdue means to have gone past the date that something was due to be paid, returned, eaten, or drunk; 'it is past the due date.'

Overdo is to do something in excess, to exaggerate, to go overboard, to go to extremes, to over indulge, to do too much of something.

Overseas-Oversees

Overseas is to be abroad in another country, across or beyond the seas.

Oversees is to watch over, to manage, to organise, to survey or to supervise.

P

Pact-Packed

Pact means an agreement, a treaty between people or countries

Packed means full to capacity, crammed, overflowing, jam-**packed**.

Packed means to have stored, boxed away, bundled or put clothes into a suitcase.

Paced-Paste

Paced is the regulation or manner of speed at which something was done; she paced herself to get the paperwork finished by a certain time.

Paced is to have walked at a certain rate or speed: he **paced** the streets quickly: she **paced** the room back and forth in a slow manner.

Paste is a smooth sticky mixture used for adhering and gluing things together.

Pail-Pale

Pail is a bucket.

Pale means lacking in colour, pallid, wan and colourless.

Palate-Pallet-Palette

Palate is the roof of the mouth.

Pallet is a movable platform used for storing, stacking or transporting goods.

Palette is a board with a thumbhole, which artists hold while they are painting; it is used to place paint on and to mix colours.

Pain-Pane

Pain is to feel hurt; it can be physical **pain** caused by injury or illness or it can be emotional **pain** and heartache.

Pane is the glass panel that is used in a window: **pane** of glass; window**pane**,

Pampas-Pampers

Pampas is a large treeless area of grassland in South America.

Pampas is a large plant with long grass stems and long feather type flowers.

Pampers is to luxuriate, spoil, overindulge, or cosset oneself or others.

Patience-Patients

Patience means tolerance, endurance, calmness or a good-nature.

Patients are people under the care of doctors, dentists, and nurses.

Passed-Past

Passed is to have gone by, to have by-**passed**, to have transferred from one place to another or from person to person; 'I **passed** the football stadium earlier: I **passed** the message on.'

Passed is to be successful in a test or exam; 'I **passed** the exam with flying colours.'

Past is time gone by, it is neither the present nor the future; it is time that has elapsed.

Pare-Pair-Pear (See also peel)

Pare means to cut off, to peel the skin of fruit, to trim the edges.

Pair is two of something, such as a pair of socks and a pair of shoes.

Pear is a fruit.

Pause-Paws

Pause is to stop momentarily, to hesitate, to linger for a moment in music, action, or speech.

Paws are the hands and feet of an animal.

Peace-Piece

Peace means quiet, tranquillity, serenity, calmness.

Piece is a smaller part of something bigger, a smaller portion or separate quantity, such as a **piece** of fruit or a piece of cake.

Peak-Peek

Peak is the highest point of something; the pointed top of a mountain is called the **peak**.

Peek is to take a quick look, to take a peep at something or a furtive glance.

Pedal-Peddle

Pedal is a foot lever, which is used for peddling a bike, driving a car and for playing the organ or piano.

Peddle is to go from place to place or house to house selling small items; 'to **peddle** your wares.'

Peal-Peel (See Pare)

Peal is the loud clanging sound of bells, as in the ringing of church bells.

Peel is the skin covering fruits such as oranges.

Peel is to remove the rind or skin from fruit and vegetables or to **peel** back a covering.

Per-Purr

Per is used in place of words such as, for, each, an, apiece, usual; or in accordance with something; 'I drove at 30 miles **per** hour: I knitted the jumper **per** instructions: I walked the dog as **per** usual.'

Purr is the humming vibratory sound a cat makes when it is content.

Perches-Purchase

Perches are usually horizontal bars that birds land on to roost, sit or rest upon, such as a pole or branches of a tree.

Perches are a type of small fish.

Purchase is to buy something; 'I am going to **purchase** a new coat.'

Peer-Pier

Peer is to gaze, scrutinise, and look closely or intently at something.

Peer means someone of equal standing, those of the same group.

Peer is a nobleman.

Pier is a large structure like a bridge that extends from the shore and over a river or sea.

Personal-Personnel

Personal refers to an individual person's private character and affairs.

Personnel are the staff of an organisation or company.

Phial-File (See File)

Phial is a small glass, cylindrical bottle used for storing liquids. (See Vial)

File is a recording of related information or data.

File is a box or folder in which papers are kept in order.

File is an orderly queue or line where people stand behind each other in single **file**.

File is a tool or implement with a coarse surface used for smoothing or shaping rough edges.

Pi-Pie

Pi in mathematics relates to a circle's circumference in relation to its diameter.

Pi is the 16th letter of the Greek alphabet.

Pie is a dish made of pastry and filled with either a savoury filling or a sweet filling, such as a chicken **pie** or an apple **pie**.

Pidgin-Pigeon

Pidgin is a simplified form of more than one language containing basic grammar and vocabulary.

Pigeon is a bird related to the Dove. It is from the *Columbidae* family.

Place-Plaice

Place is a location, an area, a particular part, position, point, or space; 'I travelled to that particular **place** in France: **place** my cup on the table: she won first **place** in the race: take your **place** in the queue.'

Plaice is a large flat fish that lives in the North Sea. Fishmongers and fish and chip shops sell **Plaice**.

Plane-Plain

Plane is short for aero**plane**.

Plane is a large flat surface or area.

Plane is a carpenter's tool used for smoothing wood.

Plain means unadorned, unattractive, simple, straightforward, obvious, and ordinary.

Plaintiff-Plaintive

Plaintiff is someone that brings a legal case against another person, the defendant, in a court of law.

Plaintive means to express sorrow, mourning, and sadness.

Please-Pleas

Please is to express politeness and good manners in the request for something; '**please** may I have your attention: **please** may I have a drink: 'yes **please** that would be nice.'

Pleas means to appeal, to request, to beseech, to beg, to give explanations or reasons in justification or apology, to make an earnest petition. To hear the **pleas** in a court of law is to plead one's case.

Plumb-Plum

Plum is a fleshy sweet fruit.

Plumb is a weight at the end of a line to measure how deep water is or to measure a straight vertical line.

Plumb is to fit or install items, such as sinks, baths, toilets, and washing machines, to a water supply.

Populace-Populous

Populace means the general population in a country; the general public and the inhabitants.

Populous means heavily crowded, overpopulated by people. Too many people or inhabitants in one place.

Pour-poor-pore

Pour is to tip liquid out of a container, to rain heavily, to flow forth freely and continuously; 'I will **pour** us a drink of lemonade: there is a down**pour** of rain expected today.'

Poor is to have very little or no money or goods. To be penniless, to be living in poverty.

Pore is the minute microscopic holes or openings in the skin through which sweat and oils pass through.

Pray-Prey

Pray is to talk to God, to offer up devotion, praise, worship, requests and pleas.

Prey is an animal that is hunted for food by another animal. Owls **prey** on mice to eat: the Tiger hunts its **prey**: the fox seized its **prey**. (See preys)

Prey is to take advantage of another person, to exploit, trick, blackmail, harass, intimidate, control or manipulate. It is to **prey** on someone.

Prey is to be worried or burdened; 'the situation started to **prey** on my mind!'

Praise-Preys

Praise is used in worship to God.

Praise is to give compliments, to express admiration, respect, and approval; to show gratitude.

Preys are animals hunted for food. (See prey).

Practice-Practise

Practice refers to the act itself or business premises: 'Dr Smith has a **practice** in the town centre where he **practice's** medicine.'

Practise is to repeat something continuously until you get the hang of it, remember it, become proficient or perfect at it.

Precedent-President

Precedent refers to something that has already happened and has set an example for the future if any similar situation arises; 'Today the court-of-Law ruled a verdict that set a **precedent** for any future rulings of a similar case.'

President is the leader and head of a state or a country.

Presents-Presence

Presents are gifts that are given, such as Christmas and birthday **presents**.

Presence is the act of being somewhere in person: 'your **presence** is required at the dinner party tonight.'

Presence is the impressive appearance, manner, or personality of a person. Someone who has a charming and charismatic personality, is said to have **presence**.

Pride-Pried

Pride refers to a person's self-respect, self-regard, standard and morals; 'I will not be dishonest as I have my **pride**: I take **pride** in my home by always keeping it clean.'

Pride is an expression of an achievement or something or someone: 'the Dunn family take great **pride** in their children: winning first prize gave Tim a sense **of pride**.'

Pride is when someone is conceited, full of self-importance, has a very high opinion of themselves and an over inflated ego.

Pride is a family of lions.

Pried is to have been nosey, to have been inquisitive about something personal: to have **pried** into someone else's affairs.

Pried is to have opened, moved, separated, or raised by exerting leverage and force; 'I **pried** the lid of the jar open as it was very stiff to undo.'

Pries-Prize (See pried)

Pries is to be nosey or to interfere in other people's business; 'she **pries** in other peoples' personal affairs, which do not concern her.'

Pries is to open, move, separate or raise something with force.

Prize is a reward for winning a contest or competition.

Prior-Prier

Prior means existing earlier in time, preceding, previous; 'I have a **prior** engagement which I made last week.'

Prior is a monk who is the head of a religious order, usually a rank below an abbot.

Prier is someone that is nosey and who interferes or meddles in other peoples' business. (See pries and pried)

Prince-Prints

Prince is a son of a king or queen.

Prints are drawings, designs, photocopies, photographs and lettering, which are transferred onto paper or other material by a printing machine.

Prints are the letters and words that appear on each page in printed publications such as books, magazines and newspapers.

Prints are copies or reproductions made of original works of art.

Principle-Principal

Principle is the moral belief, values and conduct on which a person's attitude and standards are based; 'he is a person of a strong moral **principle** concerning good manners.'

Principle refers to the basic rule, law, assumption, idea or truth on which a **principle** is based. 'The school is based on the **principle** that everyone has a right to learn.'

Principal is the head teacher in charge of colleges and universities.

Principal refers to someone who is of importance or in authority: the head of a school, a leader, the boss of a company.

Profit-Prophet

Profit is to benefit or gain financially, to make, or receive extra income by financial returns on a sale.

Prophet, someone that interprets and foretells the will of God: Moses was a **prophet** who was chosen to lead the people of Israel.

Pros-Prose

Pros is the shortened form for the word professionals. 'They are **pros** in their field of engineering.'

Pros refers to being in favour of something as opposed to anti which means against; weighing up the **pros** and cons.

Prose is the ordinary form of language either written or spoken.

Q

Quay-Key (see Key)

Quay is the place ships dock to have their cargo loaded or unloaded.

Key is a locking and unlocking metal implement shaped to fit exactly into **key**holes, doors, boxes and safes.

Key is musical note and pitch.

Key is an Island or reef, usually in the Caribbean.

Key refers to something of importance or of significance. 'That actress is the **key** player in the film.'

Quarts-Quartz

Quarts are a unit of liquid measure.

Quartz are crystallized forms of silica. Pure **quartz** crystal is known as rock crystal and is transparent. There are coloured varieties such as amethyst which is purple.

Queue-Cue (See Cue)

Queue is a line of people waiting to be served in a shop or waiting to get on a bus; it is forming an orderly line and waiting your turn.

Cue is a long stick used to play snooker or pool with.

Cue is a signal to begin or commence; when I give you the **cue** (signal) 'you may then begin.'

R

Rabbit-Rabbet

Rabbit is a long eared mammal that burrows underground; it is a cousin of the hare.

Rabbet is a groove, or recess cut in the edge of wood or cardboard to enable another piece to fit into it to form a joint.

Rain-Reign-Rein

Rain is water that is condensed into the atmosphere and falls in droplets from the clouds.

Reign is the period of time when a king or a queen is in power.

Rein is part of a horse's headgear; the **reign** is a strap which is attached to a bridle and used to guide and control the horse. (See Bridle).

Raise-Rays-Raze

Raise is to bring up, to move higher, to lift to an upper position, to rise upwards, to elevate, to increase in amount, to bring forth, to make a collection of money.

Rays are radiated beams of light or heat; the sun emits **rays**.

Raze is to destroy, to crush, to bring level with the ground; to demolish buildings.

Rap-wrap

Rap is to knock, strike lightly or sharply.

Rap is taking the blame; receiving harsh criticism; 'he took the **rap** for the crime: she took the **rap** for the job done badly by her colleague.'

Rap music is part of the hip hop culture, originating from America; it is putting words to rhythm.

Wrap is to cover, envelop, or fold paper or cloth over something to hide or protect it; to **wrap** up a present: to **wrap** a blanket around the shoulders to keep warm.

Red-Read

Red is a colour, it is one of the primary colours which are '**red**, green and blue.'

Read is to have performed the act of reading. (See read below)

Read-Reed

Read is to discern and understand the written and printed word. (See read above)

Reed is tall thin grass that grows by rivers, marshes, and streams.

Real-Reel

Real means genuine, true and not an imitation.

Real is something that is not imaginary but exists.

Reel is a round cylindrical mechanism for winding fishing lines and bobbin spools.

Reel is to sway, stagger, and fall about.

Reel is a Scottish dance.

Recede-Reseed

Recede is to move back, withdraw, or diminish.

Reseed is to replant with seed; to seed again.

Receipt-Reseat

Receipt is a written or printed proof of payment made for goods received.

Reseat is to move from one seat to another; to change seating.

Residence-Residents

Residence is the place that a person occupies, where people live and dwell.

Residents are the people that live in and reside in dwellings.

Retch-Wretch

Retch is to heave and strain when vomiting.

Wretch is a miserable, unhappy, unfortunate, or despicable person.

48

Rough-Ruff

Right- Rite-Write

Right refers to correct and true; what is just and good.

Right is the opposite of left.

Rite is a formal or religious ceremony; a customary and ritual system of practice; a **rite** of passage.

Write is to put pen or pencil to paper and form letters and words.

Ring-Wring

Ring, a small circular band of metal that is worn on the fingers. Some **rings** are set with gems such as a diamond **ring**.

Ring is a bell-like sound; the sound a phone makes is called a **ring,**

Wring is to twist compress or squeeze to extract moisture or liquid.

Role-Roll

Role is a part or character that actors and actresses play.

Roll is to turn over and over, to revolve, to wind; to rotate forward as in a wheel or a ball.

Roll is a small round bread loaf; it comes as a soft **roll** or a crusty **roll**. A ham and cheese **roll**.

Root-Route

Root is the part that a plant grows from; the **root** grows under the soil and extracts nutrients and water to feed the whole plant.

Route is the direction, road, or the way to a destination or journey.

Roe-Row

Roe are the eggs of a female fish; fish **roe**.

Row is a straight and continuous line, as in a **row** of people, a **row** of chairs or a **row** of houses.

Row is to rotate the oars back and forth in the water to propel a boat forward.

Road-Rode

Road is an open way, usually covered by tarmac, in which vehicles drive on, often with pavements on either side for pedestrians to walk on.

Rode is the past of ride; it is to have ridden in or on something; 'she **rode** her horse: **he rode** in the car: she **rode** her bike.'

Roam-Rome

Roam is to travel, move about, or wander aimlessly with no particular destination.

Rome is the capital city of Italy.

Rough-Ruff

Rough means coarse, uneven, and irregular, not smooth or level.

Rough is used to describe a person whose manner is coarse, rude, harsh, or brutal.

Ruff is a high frilled collar, worn around the neck in Elizabethan times.

Ruff is a small European fresh water fish.

Rude-Rued-Rood

Rude is to be bad mannered, insulting, crude, impolite, offensive.

Rued means to have felt regret, remorse and sorrow.

Rood is a large crucifix, a cross.

Rung-Wrung

Rung is the step on a ladder.

Wrung is past of wring; for example, to have twisted and squeezed water out of the wet towels. 'I've **wrung** the towels out.' (See Wring)

Rye-Wry

Rye is a cereal plant used for making bread and whiskey.

Wry refers to a dry, sarcastic, ironic, and mocking sense of humour.

S

Sac-Sack

Sac is a pouch shaped structure that often contains fluid such as a blister, a cyst or the bladder.

Sack is a large bag made from strong coarse material used for holding potatoes, grain, or coal.

Sack is a term used when a person loses their job; 'he got the **sack** from his job.'

Sale-Sail

Sale is selling or exchanging goods or services for money. (See sell).

Sale is when goods or services are sold at a reduced price.

Sail is the large canvass fabric on a boat that is propelled by the wind.

Sail is to travel by boat or ship.

Saw-Soar-Sore

Saw is a blade with sharp teeth used for cutting wood, metal and other hard materials.

Saw is to have looked at, to have seen, to have viewed visually with the eyes. It is the past tense of see. 'I **saw** her yesterday.' (See see)

Soar is to fly high, to move upwards in the sky.

Soar is to rise, to increase rapidly; 'the price of goods continues to **soar**.'

Sore is a tender, painful, or sensitive area, on or within the body. A **sore** throat; a cold **sore**.

Sea-See

Sea is the ocean, a large expanse of salt water.

See is to have sight and vision of the eyes. (See sight and seen).

See refers to the ability to ascertain and understand. For example, 'I **see** what you're saying, I understand.'

Sealing-Ceiling

Sealing is securing and closing something tightly, to make air tight, water proof or safe proof, such as the **sealing** of an envelope.

Ceiling the interior overhead surface of a room, an inside roof.

Seam-Seem
Seam is the line where two pieces of cloth have been sown together.
Seem is to give the appearance, impression, the assumption of something; to appear true, to reason in one's own mind; 'I **seem** to have misplaced my keys: it would **seem** reasonable to let her come with us; it may **seem** like a good idea but I'm not sure.'

Scene-Seen
Scene is a landscape, place or a view.
Scene refers to a particular area where an event took place, such as a **scene** of crime.
Scene is the stage, setting and background in a theatre for performances and plays.
Seen is to have, perceived, observed and viewed with the eyes. (See sight and see)

Scent-Sent-Cent (See cent and cents)
Scent is perfume, a fragrance, an odour, an aroma, a certain smell.
Sent is to have dispatched, issued and transmitted; to have directed to a certain location; 'the letter was **sent** yesterday: the troops have been **sent** out.'
Cent is part of the United States currency; it is 100th part of a dollar.

Senses-Census-Censors (See Censors)
Senses are what humans and animals possess, which are sight, hearing, taste, touch and smell.
Senses refers to feelings, awareness, and perception of something; 'she **senses** you like her.' (See Sense)
Census is the official count of the population.
Censors are critics authorised to remove anything offensive, unsuitable and unreasonable in films, photos, books, plays and posters.

Scents-Sense
Scents is more than one fragrance, smell, aroma and odour, (See Scent)
Sense refers to perception, awareness, discernment, a sensation, or feeling of something. (See senses).
Sense refers to common **sense**, someone with wisdom, understanding and good sound judgement.

Seed-Cede (See Cede)
Seed is a pip, stone, a germinated part of a plant that something grows from. A plant **seed**.
Seed is a top tennis player.
Cede is to give in, to yield, to surrender.

Session-Cession
Session is a meeting, a gathering, a conference, such as, a court in **session** or a group meeting.
Session refers to taking part in something active, like a music **session**, a dancing **session**, a **session** at the gym, a teaching **session**.
Cession is surrendering.

Serial-Cereal (See cereal)
Serial is something presented in instalments; it is a series of things.
Cereal is grass such as barley, corn, grain, wheat, rice and oats, they are used to make breakfast foods.

Shear-Sheer
Shear is to cut, clip, and remove hair: sheep are sheared and their wool is removed.
Sheer refers to a very steep incline.
Sheer is fine, thin, transparent material.

Shore-Sure
Shore is the land that runs along the edge of the sea; it is the beach or coastline.
Sure is to be certain, confident, without doubt, positive and affirmative; 'I am **sure** that the bus will come soon; **sure**, I can do that for you.'

Sic-Sick
Sic usually appears beside a passage of writing to mean that it is an exact copy and quotation, word for word that it has not been altered in any way.
Sick means to be ill, unwell and poorly.
Sick is another name for vomit, to vomit is to be **sick**, to throw up.

Sew-So-Sow
Sew is to stitch or darn with needle and thread. To **sew** up a tear or a hole.
So is used to express a state, manner or result implied; 'it is **so**: the product was sold out **so** I was unable to buy it: **so** what if he can't do it: **so** I said yes we can meet.'
Sow is to scatter seeds on the ground.

Sight-site-cite (See Cite)
Sight is to see, to have vision: it is the ability of seeing. (See, see and seen)
Site is a place or location, for example, a building site.
Cite is to quote from a book.
Cite is to refer to an author, passage or book.
Cite is to call upon someone to officially appear in court.

Sighed-Side
Sighed is to have let out a deep audible breath denoting relief, sadness, frustration, tiredness, or similar emotions.
Side is not in front or behind; it is to the left or the right.
Side is a sports team, squad, or line up.
Side is something **side**ways, horizontal, lateral, adjacent.

Sighs-Size
Sighs is to let out a deep audible breath. (See sighed)
Size is how big or small, long or short something is; the overall dimension.

Stationary-Stationery
Stationary means, not moving, standing still, staying in one place.
Stationery is writing materials such as paper, pens, pencils, envelopes.

T
Tale-Tail
Tale is a true or fictitious story.
Tail is the hindmost part of an animal that extends from the backbone. A dog's **tail**, a cat's **tail**.

Taut-Taught
Taut is stretched or pulled tightly, not loose or slack.
Taught is the past of teach; the tutor **taught** French lessons today.

Tea-Tee
Tea is a drink made from **tea** leaves.
Tee is the small peg, which is put in the ground for holding a golf ball.

Team-Teem
Team are a number of people or a group of people making up a side in a contest or game or in a joint venture. Such as a football **team** or a **team** of explorers.
Teem is to pour, to swarm, to be full of, in abundance. The seas **teem** with fish.

Tear-Tier
Tear (pronounced teer), is the watery fluid that comes from the eyes when you cry, as in **tear**drops.
Tier is one of a series of levels or rows; the wedding cake had three **tiers**.

Tents-Tense
Tents are portable shelters made of canvas or other waterproof material, which people use for camping.
Tense is to feel under emotional stress and strain, to be anxious, to worry, to feel nervous.
Tense is when something is stretched very tight, so that it is taut and rigid. (see Taut)
Tense is used in time, as in past **tense** and present **tense**.

Their-There-They're
Their relates to certain people and things belonging to them or themselves, for example; the neighbours have **their** relatives visiting: **their** is no room here.
There refers to, a place, a position, here, near, close by: 'go over **there**: it is in **there**: it is over **there** near the hotel: it's neither here nor **there**: are we **there** yet'?
They're is a contraction; it is a shortened word for 'they are.'

Turn-Tern

Turn is to move your body around or partly around.

Tern is a sea bird; it is related to the gull but smaller in size.

Tern is a word used to describe a set of three numbers, especially three winning numbers in the lottery.

Ton-Tun

Ton is a unit of weight, equal to 2000 pounds.

Tun is a large casket or barrel for holding and storing beer or wine.

Tract-Tracked

Tract is an area of land or water.

Tract is an organ in the body, such as the digestive **tract**.

Tracked is to have followed, trailed, pursued, observed, or monitored the movements of an animal or person.

Troop-Troup

Troop is to march or walk at a steady pace.

Troop is a gathering or group of animals or people.

Troop is the *British Military*, **a troop** of soldiers.

Troop the colour, is a ceremony carried out by parading the flag of the regiment.

Troup is a group of performers, such as a band, a group of singers, or a theatre company that travels around to different areas performing.

U

Unwanted-Unwonted

Unwanted means not wanted, not needed, not desired.

Unwonted means, not the usual, not customary, out of the ordinary.

V

Vale-Vail-Veil

Vale means valley. **Vale** is often used in poetry.

Vail is to take off and lower one's hat as a sign of respect.

Vail is a ski resort in northern Colorado.

Veil is a piece of sheer, thin, material worn over the head, shoulders and face for concealment; a **veil** is worn on the head by the bride getting married; a **veil** is part of a nun's headdress, which covers the head.

Veil means to screen, conceal, separate, or obscure; 'the road ahead was covered in a **veil** of mist: the truth is shrouded in a **veil** of mystery!'

Vane-Vain-Vein

Vane is a flat or curved blade that is propelled around by the wind or water, such as a weather **vane** and a windmill **vane**.

Vain is to have a very high opinion of oneself, to be conceited, arrogant, full of pride.

Vain refers to futile, useless, or unsuccessful attempts at something; 'they tried in **vain** to get the car to work but it was useless.'

Vein is a blood vessel which carries blood from parts of the body back to the heart.

Verses-Versus

Verses are the lines in poems or songs.

Versus is against, in opposition to, in contrast to. In sport it's one team **versus** another such as England **versus** Italy in Football.

Vial-Vile

Vial is a small cylindrical bottle also known as a phial (see Phial).

Vile is disgusting, repulsive, nauseating, offensive and despicable: the act of murder is **vile**: that sickening smell is **vile**: that disgusting behaviour is **vile**.

W

Wade-Weighed

Wade is to walk through shallow water.

Weighed is to have used scales for determining the weight of something. (See Weigh)

Way-Weigh-Whey

Way is the customary manner, style, habit or method of doing things; 'she did it her **way**: they have done it that **way** for years.'

Way refers to possibility; 'there must be another **way** or there is a better **way** of doing things.

Way is a route, path, distance, direction; 'you must go that **way** to get to the town: the **way** to get there is to follow that path.'

Weigh is to use scales to determine the weight of something (see weighed).

Whey is the watery part of milk that separates from the curd.

Wait-Weight

Wait is to be in expectation of something, to bide time, to delay or postpone: 'my appointment was cancelled, so now I have to **wait** another three weeks: please **wait** there.'

Weight is the quantity, lightness, or heaviness of mass or matter.

War-Wore

War is armed conflict between opposing groups within a country or different countries fighting against each other.

Wore is the past of wear; 'I **wore** my best dress last week: I **wore** protective headgear when I went onto the building site.'

Warn-Worn (See Wear)

Warn is to advise ahead of time, to inform, or to make aware in advance of impending trouble or danger.

Worn is the past of wear; 'that dress has already been **worn**.'

Worn is diminished, deteriorated, wasted away, frayed, threadbare, shabby, tatty; 'his shoes are shabby and **worn** out.'

Worn refers to tired; 'after working hard all day I am **worn** out: after her illness, her face looked tired and **worn**.'

Waist-Waste

Waist is the narrow part of the body between the ribs and the hips.

Waste is discarded garbage or rubbish. Anything unwanted, unused, surplus, left over or spare, anything in excess of what is needed is **waste**.

Waste is to not make use of a good opportunity, or something useful. 'A **waste** of a good opportunity.'

Waste is to squander money or indulge oneself on useless items.

Waste is to become feeble and emaciated due to a disease or illness. To **waste** away.

Whale-Wail

Whale is a large sea mammal.

Wail is a high pitch cry.

Wax-Whacks

Wax secreted by bees and also known as **bee**swax, is a fatty, oily substance that is used to make candles.

Wax is produced in the ears. It is secreted from the glands that line the canal of the outer ear.

Whacks are strikes, slaps, clouts, or forceful blows.

Weak-Week

Weak is to have little or no strength, power or control; to be feeble.

Week is made up of the seven days; Monday, Tuesday, Wednesday, Thursday, Friday, Saturday and Sunday. (See days)

Weave-We've

Weave is intertwined and interlaced thread, yarn or material.

Weave is to zigzag, twist and turn to avoid obstacles and obstructions. **Weave** in and out of the traffic.

We've is a contraction or a shortened word for 'we have'.

Weed-We'd

Weed is a wild plant such as a dandelion or stinging nettle. To **weed** is to remove or pull up out of the ground any wild plants that grow amongst cultivated plants.

We'd is a contraction or a shortened word for, we had, we would, we should.

We-Wee

We is used to refer to yourself and one or more other persons or people; 'we went to the cinema and **we** both enjoyed the movie.'

Wee is a Scottish term meaning very small or little.

Wee is an informal word for urinating.

Weld-Welled

Weld is to fuse or join together pieces of metal, plastic, or other materials by heating to boiling point first.

Weld is a plant of southern Europe, which gives off a yellow dye.

Welled is to have been overcome by emotion, wanted to cry, to have filled up, and spilt over.

Wheel-Wheal-We'll

Wheel is a round object that rotates in a circular motion on an axle; the **wheels** on a car are what make it move.

Wheal is a raised area of skin, which is sore, itches, or irritates, it is also known as a welt.

We'll is a contraction or a shorter word for we will or we shall.

Where-Ware-Wear

Where refers to what place, from what source, at which point, at which place or position; 'where are we going: **where** did that come from: would you like to know **where** I bought my bicycle? Your keys are **where** you left them: **where** did you hear that?'

Ware is items for sale; the salesman went from house to house peddling his **wares**.

Ware is a specific type of article, such as, crystal **ware** and silver **ware**.

Wear is to have on clothes, jewellery or any other covering or adornment on the head or body.

Wear is to display certain facial expressions such as; 'she **wears** a smile: he **wears** a frown.'

Wear is deterioration, scuffing, corrosion, erosion, friction: It is to **wear** away.

Wear well refers to something that lasts and does not **wear** out quickly or easily.

Wet-Whet

Wet means soaked, drenched, saturated, moistened or damp with water or other liquids.

Wet refers to raining, drizzly, showery, and damp weather. **Wet** weather.

Whet means to stimulate and excite, to increase desire or interest in something; 'this will **whet** your appetite when I tell you what I'm cooking: I have snippets of information that will **whet** your curiosity.'

Weather-Whether

Weather refers to the climatic and atmospheric condition of the day, such as sun, rain, wind or snow.

Whether is used to express doubt, enquiry, alternatives, choices; 'I doubt **whether** he will come: I'll find out **whether** or not the dog belongs to her: I am going to do it **whether** you like it or not: the choice is yours **whether** or not you take the job.'

Which-Witch

Which refers to what kind, what one, a choice, a representation. '**Which** one is it? Pick **which** one you want: **which** would you prefer: we went to Italy **which** was fantastic.'
Witch is a woman that practices magic. In fairy tales, a **witch** is portrayed as wearing a black pointed hat and long cloak, riding a broomstick.

While-Wile

While is used in, during this time, a time period, a contrast, a phase, duration. 'She visited for a **while**: **while** I was waiting I did a crossword puzzle: **while** you are in Italy I recommend visiting Salerno.'
Wile means, sly, cunning, devious; to entice, beguile, to lure, to trick, to set a trap.
Wile away, is to do something to pass the time. It is to **wile** away the time.

Wine-Whine

Wine is an alcoholic drink made from fermented grapes.
Whine is a whimper, a cry or a grizzling noise: an annoying whinging, moaning or complaining tone of voice.
Whine is a high-pitched cry that dogs make.

Whirl-Whorl

Whirl is to rotate rapidly, to spin around to twizzle and twirl.
Whorl is a spiral shape, a swirl, a vortex; something that is twisted and shaped like a coil.

Whole-Hole

Whole means, entire, complete, total, the **whole** number, the full amount and quantity, uncut, in one piece.
Hole is a cavity, an aperture, a gap, a hollow area, an opening. My sock has a **hole** in it.

Whose-Who's

Whose is the possessive of who and whom, for example; '**whose** bag is that; **whose** drawing will be the best?'
Who's is a contraction or a shorter word for 'who is.'

Woe-Whoa

Woe is grief, trouble, or great sorrow; for example, '**woe** is me, I am in great distress.'
Whoa is a command to stop a horse.

Wood-Would

Wood comes from trees, which are used to make furniture, paper and other items.
Wood is an area that has an abundance or thicket of trees. A forest; a **wood**land.
Would is past of 'will', to give advice, an expression of an opinion, desire or request. 'If I were you I **would** go there; 'I **would** have done it yesterday but I was busy; I **would** love to be on holiday right now; **would** you make me a cup of tea please; she **would** say that.'

Worst-Wurst
Worst is the poorest of conditions, the poorest quality of something, the lowest standard, the most severe or extreme conditions of an illness, the most unpleasant personality of someone or their behaviour, the vilest, the nastiest, the foulest. The most terrible or unpleasant situation. It is the opposite of best.
Wurst is a large sausage eaten in Germany and Austria.

Wreak-Reek
Wreak is to cause severe damage, to inflict harm, to exact revenge. She was angry and wanted to **wreak** revenge for losing her job: earthquakes **wreak** havoc in their midst.
Reek is a strong offensive or foul stink, smell or odour.

Y
Yoke-Yolk
Yoke is a wooden crossbar, harness, or frame, which encircles the neck; it joins two or more oxen together to make them pull at the same time.
Yoke is a frame, which sits on a person's shoulders for carrying buckets or baskets.
Yoke is part of a garment on which the rest of the garment hangs from; usually around the neck, chest and shoulders area.
Yoke together means to join, unite, or link.
Yoke is oppression, repression, burden, a heavy load to carry emotionally and mentally; the people were under the **yoke** of a tyrannical ruler. He bore the **yoke** of his infirmities.'
Yolk is the yellow middle part of the egg, it is rich in fat and protein which nourishes the developing embryo.

Yew-You-Ewe
Yew is a tree.
You refers to one or more person or persons; 'I love **you**: **you** did well: **you** are all going to the party: I'm so proud of all of **you**.'
Ewe is a female sheep.

Your-You're-Yore
Your belongs to the person or persons being addressed, it can also refer to **your**self, for example, 'It melts **your** heart to hear the children sing: I am **your** friend: what is **your** job title? They are not **your** average type of law breakers.'
Your is used to address people with certain titles, such as '**your** Excellency, **your** highness, **your** majesty.'
You're is a contraction or a short word for 'you are'.
Yore means time gone by, long ago.

Yule-You'll
Yule from **yule**-tide, is an old-fashioned word for Christmas-time.
You'll is a contraction or a short word for, 'you will, you shall, you all'.

Some examples of homonyms
Words that are spelled the same but with different meanings.

Address: A place where someone lives.
Address: A formal speech given to an audience.
Address: An attempt to deal with or tackle a difficult situation or problem.

Bank: An institution that offers financial services.
Bank: The edge of a river; the riverbank.

Barge: A large boat.
Barge: To move clumsily, to push past people.

Bill: A man's name.
Bill: A bird's beak.
Bill: An invoice or a charge for a service used requiring paymnet.

Box: A cardboard or wooden container.
Box: To fight with fists.

Canine: Dogs.
Canine: teeth.

Contract: A contract is a formal agreement, between two or more persons or companies.
Contract: Muscles that become tighter, shorter and are drawn together to allow the movement of parts of the body
Contract: Is to catch an illness or disease by picking it up from someone or somewhere else.

Key: A metal implement shaped to fit exactly into keyholes to lock and unlock doors, boxes and safes.
Key: A low-lying Island usually in the Caribbean.

Lead: (pronounced Leed). To go first, to lead a person or a group to show a person or people the way to somewhere.
Lead: (pronounced Led). A soft bluish heavy material used as slates for roofs. Also found in lead pencils.
Lead: (pronounced Leed). A long leather, plastic, or nylon strap used for walking a dog.

Live: (pronounced Liv). To exist;
Live: Charged with electricity. A live band playing

Nut: A hard fruit
Nut: a small metal ring used with a bolt

Object: Is something that does not move but can be seen and touched.
Object: The main purpose or aim.
Object: To disagree.

Pen: A writing or drawing implement.
Pen: An enclosure in which animals are kept.

Perch: A resting place for birds.
Perch: A freshwater fish.

Pine: An evergreen tree.
Pine: to grieve, to miss, to feel great longing for someone or something.

Polish: (pronounced poll-ish) To shine or make smooth by rubbing.
Polish: (pronounced pole-ish) A person from the country Poland and the language spoken.

Pound: The old unit of weight
Pound: To beat or crush heavily, to pound your fists
Pound: An enclosure where animals are kept

Pool: A swimming pool, a puddle of water, a small amount of liquid.
Pool: A billiard game similar to snooker.

Quack: The sound ducks make.
Quack: A person with no medical qualifications posing as a doctor.

Read: To discern and understand the written and printed word
Read: (pronounced red), is to have done the reading.

Rob: A name usually short for Robert
Rob: to steal

Rose: Past tense of rise
Rose: A fragrant flower

Row: To propel a boat using oars
Row: A line of people or things

Seal: Is an aquatic mammal that eats fish.
Seal: Is to make something secure, watertight, to join something together.
Seal: Wax with an authentic mark stamped into it is a seal.

Tear: (pronounced teer). Fluid that comes from the eyes when you cry; as in teardrops.
Tear: (pronounced tair). Is to shred, to rip.

Tip: To push or tilt
Tip: To give some money for a service. (To tip a Waiter)
Tip: To give someone advice or information.

Trunk: Elephants long nose
Trunk: A large storage box
Trunk: The Main part of a tree
Trunk: The human body (not the arms, legs, neck, or head)
Trunk: The boot of a car
Trunks: Swimming shorts

Well: To be in good health
Well: A Large deep hole containing water

Wound: (pronounced wowned) Is to have turned, or twisted something in a spiral movement.
Wound: (pronounced woond) Is an injury, open sore, cut, or damage to skin or tissue.